I0463233

5 Rules of Consumer Engagement

TOOLS FOR YOUR MARKETING TOOLBOX

By Dr. Sam Cohen, Sigal Kremer, and Melinda Wooten

Cover and Inside Illustrations by
Ian Spence

Contents

Foreword

In a world where the average consumer walks past a long wall of flat screen TVs priced similarly and can't tell the difference between one versus the other, how do you influence brand choice?

As marketers, advertisers and creatives, our job often involves crafting messages that hone preference and drive sales. Sometimes we get lucky and work on a brand with a discernible and important competitive advantage to consumers. But often we work in categories that are increasingly crowded and/or filled with products that have little perceptible difference from competition (at least in the consumer's mind).

That's when we dig deeper to uncover the reason our brand should be chosen above all others. We prioritize our messaging strategy, bring it to life and then try not to cringe when we expose it to consumers, holding our breath as they pick apart the communication for what seem small, inconsequential reasons, but add up to deal breakers.

Wouldn't it be nice to refine your message before you get to the cringing stage by using a set of psychological principles translated into English?

Wait a minute. Psychology? That's heavy stuff. But it doesn't have to be if you have a psychology-to-marketing dictionary, which allows you to transition from high level psychological theory to in the trenches advice. For example:

- ***Psychological Diagnosis****: A brand that can uniquely assist individuals in negotiating powerful subconscious needs and wishes, while avoiding internal conflicts/pitfalls, will be much more successful in creating a meaningful connection with consumers.*

- ***Translation***: *A brand that strikes an emotional chord while communicating – without alienating – will fly off the shelves, while those that don't can't be given away.*

Whether you're selling automobiles or garden gloves, fast food or blood pressure medication, striking a deep emotional chord is essential to the success of your brand. Your challenge is to uncover these distinct, salient, subconscious consumer needs and wishes and use them to your advantage – in branding, packaging and advertising. The good news is you don't have to get an advanced degree in psychology to do so.

The Psychological Origins of Our 5 Rules
By Dr. Samuel Cohen, psychotherapist

In the mid-1990s, I heard anecdotally about the application of psychological principles to the marketing realm and was intrigued. I routinely used a range of techniques in my practice based on relationship building, behavior, dialogue and communication changes designed to help the patient reach their full potential or cope with problems in life. And like any other American, I was in love with advertising! A combination of the two seemed a match made in heaven.

Not long after my interest was piqued, I was asked to view a set of advertising focus groups for Kiwi Shoe Polish and provide perspective on consumer reaction. In the TV ad, the Kiwi bird was playing the part of a drill sergeant, while the shoes were the soldiers. The ad begins with a Kiwi bird yelling at shoes that are at attention, telling them they don't shine. He implies the shoes are a disgrace. The ad was not well received.

- ***Psychological Diagnosis:*** *The Kiwi bird's aggression unintentionally crossed personal boundaries, triggering fears of violation and abuse. Viewers in the groups rejected the brand due to what is called identification with the aggressor – erecting staunch barriers against a perceived attack.*
- ***Translation:*** *Although the ad was supposed to be humorous many felt it to be threatening. Think about it. Would you feel comfortable with a bird squawking at your feet?*

This led to a call from an ad agency, asking me to uncover why a radio ad for Molson Beer was so successful. The ad involved a man and a woman involved in a flirtatious, yet humorous, conversation.

- **Psychological Diagnosis:** *Molson was able to unconsciously relieve men of the performance anxiety often associated (real or otherwise) with beer consumption by not resorting to stereotypical gender role behaviors.*
- **Translation:** *Listeners wished to be the quick-witted man – drinking Molson beer and retaining control of themselves in all resulting situations.*

As I worked in this emerging field, I began developing the 5 Rules of Engagement model that incorporated the critical subconscious needs, wishes and anxieties of what drives human behavior to the evaluation of communication. Consistently, I could point to one or more of these rules as a reason communication succeeded or failed, as well as use these principles to help refine messaging to improve its impact.

And as happens when any discipline blends with another, I saw a need for a translator fluent in both psychology and marketing.

Developing Communication that Connects on a Deeper Level
By Sigal Kremer and Melinda Wooten, marketing researchers

We were part of the consumer insight team working on a brand that had strong brand definition/awareness but lived in a crowded field with little brand differentiation recognized by users. We had identified functional, intellectual and emotional benefits. But when translated into television advertising, the campaign wasn't moving sales (other than conservative bumps based on retailer promotion/display when we were on air). We needed to look at things on a deeper level if we wanted to make significant impact in the marketplace.

In partnership with Dr. Sam, using techniques very similar to the tools in this book, we dug further into the emotions we had previously identified to their subconscious roots – the needs, wishes and conflicts that were triggered (or not) by our brand and its messaging. This insight allowed our brand to jump past the competition because we could talk about it and show it in a different way, a deeper way, a way that made a more powerful connection with the consumer.

Intrigued by the process, we founded KW Strategems, a full service research firm that specializes in consumer research identifying deep emotional drivers and incorporating that into strategic implications. Soon after its launch, Dr. Sam approached us about operating as a translator for the 5 Rules of Engagement.

About This Book

The goal of this book is to help marketers maximize their brand communications by achieving a deeper emotional bond with their consumer. It's a handy quick guide of five rules that will help you use the binoculars of a psychologist without obtaining a psychology degree.

---

5 Rules of Consumer Engagement

Rule 1: *Getting Into Empathic Attunement*

Rule 2: *Pulling the Trigger*

Rule 3: *Supporting Ego Boundaries*

Rule 4: *Respecting Identity Structures*

Rule 5: *Providing the Good Fit*

Introduction
Consumer Behavior Refresher

Before we dive deeper into translations, there are a few terms you'll need to be familiar with to successfully use this book.

Consumer purchase decisions are made up of two components: *the intellectual component (the mind) and the emotional component (the heart).* Can you market to only one and be successful? Rarely.

Think of it this way. We sometimes refer to people as being "right brained" or "left brained." That's not possible. The two work in nearly seamless tandem, because together they more fully address a person's needs (conscious and subconscious). It's just that one may be more dominant than the other.

The same applies to the purchase decision process. Our intellectual component operates simultaneously with the emotional component, but they are influenced differently.

- The *intellectual* component, our mind, is operating in reality. Psychologists often refer to it as conscious, secondary process thinking or our outer reality.

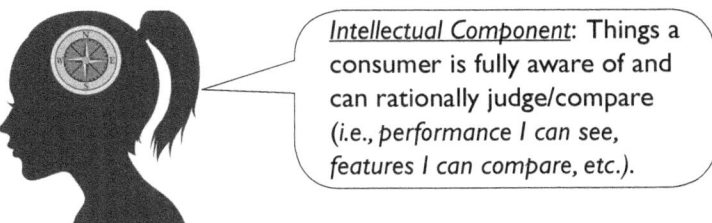

Intellectual Component: Things a consumer is fully aware of and can rationally judge/compare (*i.e., performance I can see, features I can compare, etc.*).

- *The emotional component, our heart, operates in reality combined with illusion/fantasy or wish fulfillment. Psychologists often refer to it as subconscious, primary process thinking or our inner reality.*

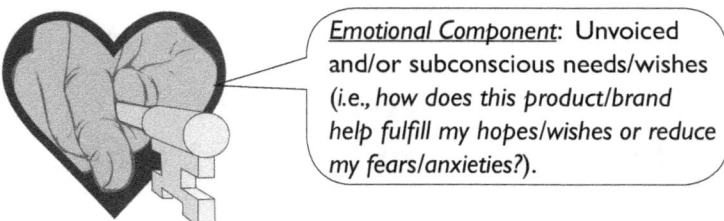

Emotional Component: Unvoiced and/or subconscious needs/wishes (*i.e., how does this product/brand help fulfill my hopes/wishes or reduce my fears/anxieties?*).

An emotional connection is essential to the success of any brand. A brand that can meet intellectual needs and uniquely assist individuals in negotiating powerful subconscious needs/wishes — while avoiding internal conflicts/pitfalls — will be much more successful in creating a meaningful connection with consumers.

Chart of Emotional and Intellectual Components

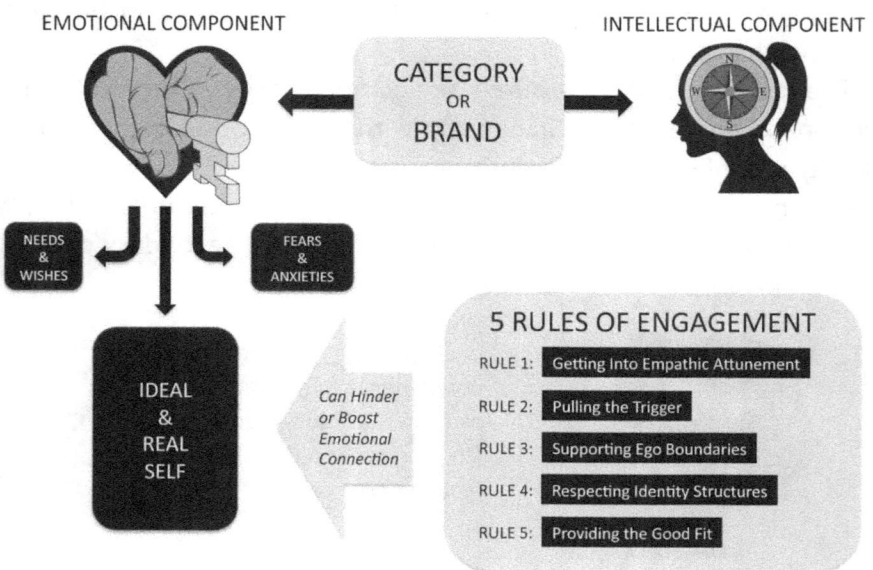

CHAPTER I
Getting into Empathic Attunement

"People will forget what you said. People will forget what you did.
But people will never forget how you made them feel."
Bonnie Jean Wasmund

In this Chapter

- ➤ What is Empathic Attunement?
- ➤ Breaking down the concept
- ➤ Examples
- ➤ How to put your idea to the test

We've all felt empathy for someone else at one time or another:

- ✓ *We wince when someone hits their finger with a hammer.*
- ✓ *We feel joy when the athlete we're rooting for wins a race.*
- ✓ *We feel fear of the unknown when someone is diagnosed with cancer.*

Today, a fast-paced lifestyle leads to less time for traditional relationships. Luckily, personal connections to people, places and things can be made through a variety of sources, not just through face-to-face interaction or through traditional advertising.

Regardless of how your message is conveyed, if a consumer feels that a brand understands them on some level, the brand has connected. The door is open to establishing interest, trust, preference and, ultimately, loyalty.

What is Empathic Attunement?

In Psychological Terms

Empathic Attunement: the capacity to think and feel oneself into the inner life of another person. (Kohut 1984)

Empathic Attunement is the psychological construct that says you identify with someone else emotionally. Achieving Empathic Attunement with the consumer can subconsciously trigger brand trust.

Empathy is established with more than verbal cues.

Empathy is developed during the early phase of our toddler years (Mahler, 1975). A baby or toddler who cannot verbalize their needs/wants tries to communicate with their parents through other means (facial expressions, body language, primal noises). We learn early that with multiple avenues of expression we can establish a connection and be understood. Therefore, we look for cues beyond the verbal as we decipher stimuli. As marketers, we must manage and control multiple, complex or confusing messages/stimuli so that we don't block the emotional connection.

Have you explored your consumers' emotional frequency? Do you know what their aspirations are? Do you know what triggers their anxiety

Just like accurately dialing into a radio station's frequency, the connection consumers have with your brand can greatly deepen if the brand is Empathically Attuned to their emotional frequency. This leads to a sense of trust and affinity toward the brand and a deeper brand meaning, which may, in turn, lead to brand purchase and increased loyalty. Essentially:

✓ *If Brand X knows me, I trust them to solve my problems.*

✓ *If Brand X knows me, I believe they can enhance me in some way.*

What is Empathic Attunement?
Translation in Everyday Terms

Empathic Attunement is about connections. If you connect with someone or something you feel that you aren't alone, that someone understands what you've gone through or what you fear or aspire to. We see empathic attunement at work, for example, when a soldier reenlists in order to remain connected to his army buddies. It's also why many people desire a friend or family member be with them when seeing a doctor about a diagnosis – in order to feel emotionally supported.

Empathy: being aware of/ sensitive to, under-standing and/or having vicariously lived the feelings, thoughts and experiences of another without them explicitly being communicated. (Webster Dictionary, 2009)

Look at the popularity of the book and subsequent movie "Marley & Me". Millions identified with the joys and tribulations of having a dog. Observe the public's fascination with tragedies that could occur in their own backyard and how that leads to increased news coverage. Note the way Barak Obama's campaign and election captured the hopes and imagination of a nation, validating the belief that you can achieve anything if you set your mind to it.

The power of a connection can influence brand interaction as deeply as it does a personal connection. In fact, brands can often substitute for the longed for personal connection or the outcome that one would hope to receive from a personal connection.

A woman from Toronto came to visit a friend in California. On her wish list? A trip to Target. She'd seen the store's television ads, but wanted to experience this store first hand.

Breaking Down the Rule
Making it work for you

Many companies strive to understand the needs and behaviors of their consumers, whether through traditional research methods or newer psychological hybrids. These insights are used to develop or refine the marketing mix. Adding Empathic Attunement to the marketer's toolbox increases the power and effectiveness of communication so that your consumers have a sense that you understand them.

In order to create a connection with the consumer, marketers need to understand the consumer's state of mind and what drives them to the category, product and brand on three levels.

Tuning into Empathy
by identifying:
• Needs
• Wishes
• Anxieties

At the Functional level

✓ Need: *What is the need? Why am I coming to the category?*

At the Emotional level

✓ Wish: *What I want it to do for me. What hopes/aspirations do I have?*

At the Subconscious level

✓ Anxiety: *What anxiety is associated with the purchase/brand/category that can act as a barrier to opinion/trial/use?*

These empathic drivers are not mutually exclusive and may exist on their own. For example, a person that is in the market for a new car might enter the category with multiple – and sometimes conflicting - drives:

> **Need:** *car broke down, need transportation (functional)*
>
> **Wish:** *express my personality (emotional)*
>
> **Anxiety:** *fear of the hassle and pressure that involves buying a new car, fear of failure to obtain a "good deal", fear of being able to afford it (subconscious)*

The brand must become sensitive not just to the rational *need* behind the purchase (need for a car), but also the subconscious *wishes* (express my personality) and *anxieties* (avoid hassle/pressure/ stress). If communication is not made to address these key drivers, then consumer connection, brand meaning and purchase interest are weakened.

Empathic Hierarchy

For many products/categories, one driver becomes more salient than the others and a hierarchy of importance is developed. A need might supersede a wish and overcome the anxiety associated with using a product/service, but the wish and anxiety remain.

How do your consumers prioritize their drivers? Does it differ by subgroup?

Empathic Targeting

To make things even more challenging for the marketer, different consumer segments may simultaneously have differing drivers and/or driver hierarchies. For example, a graduate student commuting to the city every day might be more interested in gas mileage and car length (wanting a short car so he can park anywhere) than a retired businessman in Florida who craves the safety and comfort of a larger sedan. Marketers must have a clear view of who their targets are, and where, if at all, their drives and hierarchies overlap and differ.

Watch Out: Violating or abandoning anxiety triggers can alienate one target versus the other. How much of a risk are you willing to take?

Brands that Made it Work

In the 1990's, *Saturn* was launched with an ad campaign that focused on the simplicity of buying a Saturn car. Saturn identified that the subconscious issue with buying cars was stress and intimidation. The campaign addressed these negative triggers and positioned Saturn as the dealership that treated car buyers as individuals.

Saturn tagline: "A Different Kind of Company, A Different Kind of Car."

Since the 1970's, *Alka-Seltzer's* brand messaging has consistently been about overindulging. Why have they been successful for so long? The brand understands that we all lose control sometimes when something desirable is in front of us. Alka-Seltzer is there to soothe us and bring us back in

Alka Seltzer tagline: "I can't believe I ate the whole thing."

balance. The ads are often done in a playful way rather than in a censorious tone: we understand you and we aren't going to put you down.

In an effort to support a new product introduction of a morning breakfast pastry, we conducted research to uncover underlying subconscious issues for moms in the morning. The project found that morning can be chaotic when trying to get everyone out of the house, fueled both physically and emotionally. Moms are looking to provide a good start to the morning for their family without being seen as an archetypal "witch". This gets the day off to a good beginning and makes positive connections.

- ✓ **Need**: *Mom has responsibility to feed physically and emotionally*
- ✓ **Wish**: *Provide a home cooked breakfast*
- ✓ **Anxiety:** *Get the day off to a wrong start, be a "witch"*

Pillsbury created a TV ad where a mom heats up breakfast (symbolic of baking from scratch). The aroma of breakfast drifts upstairs and catches the family's attention. They run downstairs with a smile and the morning starts out positively. Mom doesn't need to yell to get her family out of bed and moving, thus avoiding becoming the witch to her family. Everyone leaves the house in a good mood after first refueling physically (good breakfast) and emotionally (positive bonding with family/mom before separating).

Advertising Hampered without Empathic Attunement

The Infiniti car brand was launched in the United States in 1990. To create brand awareness, TV was used with Zen-influenced spots that focused on nature, but never showed the actual car. The team thought that they could create attunement with the consumer by just talking about the car. Contrary to their hopes, the campaign hurt the brand launch. Why? Subconsciously the ads triggered abandonment and thus a lack of attunement.

The ad told consumers that Infiniti exists, but not exactly what it was. As news spread that Infiniti was a car, this triggered subconscious anxiety because not enough questions about it were answered. What did it look like? Did the appearance/image fit with consumer identity? What were the functional benefits/features? Where could it be purchased? How much was it? These questions limited the connection before the car ever hit the market.

In 1988, the Democrat's choice to run for President against George H.W. Bush was Michael Dukakis. Initially, Dukakis led in the polls. Then the Democrats decided to show that Dukakis was a strong commander-in-chief, an aspect that resonated with many voters. The resulting campaign used the image of Dukakis sitting in a tank wearing an overly-large helmet. The effect of the image was opposite of their goal. It unintentionally portrayed Dukakis as small and incompetent, instead of being attuned to the nation's need to find a strong leader.

Getting into Empathic Attunement

Reviewing Rule #1

- **Psychology:** Empathic Attunement is the capacity to think and feel oneself into the inner life of another person.
- **Translation:** Empathic Attunement is about connections. If you connect with someone or something (i.e., a brand) you feel that you aren't alone, that someone understands what you've gone through or what you fear or aspire to.

Using Rule #1

Only by a brand helping a consumer to feel understood and that their needs, wishes and anxieties are known and supported, can a brand hope to make a lasting connection with their consumer. Evaluate your brand proposition and advertising by putting yourself in your target's shoes. Does your brand proposition/communication:

1. *Establish the feeling that the brand understands the consumer or segment?*
2. *Prioritize the meeting of needs, wishes and anxieties in line with your target?*
3. *Provide cues (both verbally and visually) that align with your consumer's sense of self?*
4. *Address an important concern, fear or anxiety without overwhelming the consumer?*

CHAPTER 2
Pulling the Trigger

"We cannot wish for what we know not." Voltaire

In this Chapter

➤ Trigger a Need, Wish or Anxiety
➤ Breaking down the concept
➤ Examples
➤ How to put your idea to the test

Our world is littered with good products that failed because they did not fill a need, wish or anxiety or they failed to communicate the need or wish effectively to trigger interest and, ultimately, purchase. Do you remember these short-lived product introductions?

✓ **Clairol Look of Buttermilk**. *This shampoo was introduced in test markets in 1974 but left many women perplexed. Why would they want their hair to look like buttermilk?*

✓ **Ben-Gay Aspirin.** *In the 1970's, Pfizer, the makers of Ben-Gay, introduced aspirin tablets under the Ben-Gay brand. They thought that with the kind of brand recognition they had they could sweep the market. But their aspirin offered nothing new or beneficial to consumers* *and may have triggered taste anxiety associated with Ben-Gay's strong aroma.*

Ideally, you want your communication to be noticed and trigger a response of *"Hey, that's just what I've been looking for."* Or *"I could use that."* Not *"I don't need that."* Or *"Why do I need more of the same?"*

What is a Trigger?
In Psychological Terms

Psychological principle
The need for stimulus – the striving and excitement surrounding anything new, better or meeting an unmet need, wish or fantasy. Referred to as stimulus hunger. (Glanzer, 1953)

Humans have a basic, constantly evolving need for physical and emotional supplies. Everyone is looking for something: love, wealth, glory, comfort, safety, etc. People are naturally dissatisfied with the status quo and they are on the lookout either consciously or unconsciously for something that is a better value, a better performer or something that makes them look or feel better about themselves. This is called stimulus hunger, which creates opportunity for a marketer.

There are numerous needs theories and models. Maslow's Hierarchy of Needs is probably the most famous example, identifying five basic needs, but prioritizing those needs logically, such that higher needs are presumably not satisfied until lower needs are met. However, consumers don't always behave logically and part of that may be explained by the strength and accuracy of a product's trigger.

What is a Trigger?
Translation In Everyday Terms

Triggering a need, wish or anxiety gives your product a reason for being <u>and</u> a reason for being the right product for the consumer. Whether your product solves a problem, eases an anxiety or fulfills a fantasy, communicating this attracts the consumer.

Need: a lack of something requisite, desirable, or useful. (Webster Dictionary, 2009)

Triggering can be as loud and in your face as the products Bill Mays pitched (OxiClean, Fix it! Scratch Remover, Mighty Putty, etc.) or as subtly quiet as Corona Beer. Did you laugh when you saw the commercial for the Snuggie (Snuggie™ Blanket… the Blanket with Sleeves!)? The marketers did. They recognized a need, marketed it during a peak holiday period in a recession and laughed with their three million in sales all the way to the bank.

Wish: to have a desire: want; to make a wish. (Webster Dictionary, 2009)

Anxiety: painful or apprehensive uneasiness of mind, usually over an impending or anticipated ill. (Webster Dictionary, 2009)

Breaking Down the Rule
Making it work for you

If you don't trigger a need (real or imagined) or convey how to avoid anxiety, no matter how good your product or service, the message will be lost. However, if you do trigger a need – even if it is one as seemingly inconsequential as keeping your arms warm while you change the channel on television – you'll hit the bulls-eye. Who among us could predict that teeth whitening would grow to a $240 million dollar category? (Nielsen, 2008) Or that prepared wipes that can be used for anything from wiping your baby's bottom to wiping your 4-wheel drive baby's wheels would hit a need for convenience to the tune of roughly $2 billion? (Reuters, 2009)

Explore reasons to use your product and the triggers that indicate it needs to be used.

Where are your competitors or the category weak? Can your brand own a trigger?

Often the secondary/newer brand must establish a strong trigger, strong enough to break the ritual of product/brand loyalty. When Sure® underarm deodorant conveyed the message that ones' underarms could be exposed (an action that

can cause shame if you aren't properly protected), they unconsciously triggered concerns about the ineffectiveness of competitive brands. The combination of the message and the brand name *Sure* provided a powerful trigger of guaranteed protection. Providing this type of emotional guarantee leaves consumers feeling more confident and relaxed, reinforcing loyalty while creating a crack in the market leader's armor and reducing the risk of switching brands.

If something about your communication isn't working, delve into worries/anxieties related to the situation you depict.

Sometimes the marketer must introduce anxiety to position their product as the one to relieve that anxiety. However, it is important when triggering anxiety in the consumer that they never feel overwhelmed, as this initiates defenses for protection. When DuPont launched a new type of blanket that could restore ones' body temperature back to normal when exposed to great heat or fire, they hoped to trigger anxiety and a call to action by showing a home on fire. We tested the ad and found DuPont triggered overwhelming anxiety by reminding people of the vulnerability of their homes and loved ones. Consumers thought the ad was effective, yet no one remembered that DuPont was the sponsor. They repressed the name, in part due to too much fear and anxiety being triggered.

Brands that Made it Work

It's the end of the work day. You're setting the table for dinner, trying to transition from the pressures of the day to whatever the night holds. Are you there yet? Or does it take something more to shed the cares of the day and relax? In 2001, the Bella Sera Winery was successful in capturing the need to transition from the work day to personal time at home and positioning Bella Sera as the wine to fill that need. Their ad was successful in triggering this need in only a few frames using emotive music, the soft imagery of twilight and wine raised around a table of friends.

From 2008 to 2010, a classic war was waged in television advertising between Macintosh and PC software giant, Microsoft. Both campaigns were effective at triggering weaknesses with their competition in a way that was palatable.

- ✓ **Macintosh** *created a campaign with two characters that personified the Mac (straightforward, hip) and the PC (a self-deprecating used car salesman). The "Get a Mac" campaign points out the advantages of their system over a PC – no virus worries, no complicated operating system, easy networking, etc.*

- ✓ **Microsoft** *countered with their "I'm a PC" campaign which featured real life PC users showing the world how easy it was to use a PC. The landmark ad being "I'm Four and a Half", where a four and a half year old downloads a picture of her goldfish to her PC, edits it and then emails it to her parents.*

Advertising Hampered without a Strong Trigger

In order to play it safe, companies sometimes draw on pop culture references for advertising content, rather than triggering a need. Such was the case of SoBe's 2008 "Thrillicious" spot, featuring Naomi Campbell and a herd of colorful CGI lizards, who danced to Michael Jackson's Thriller after drinking SoBe. Being a second entry

in the category (after the hugely successful Vitamin Water, which used celebrities and humor in their campaign), SoBe may have benefited from a more needs-based approach.

In 2009, Cottonelle ran an ad for its toilet paper equating a day at the spa with using its product. Although undoubtedly there is a segment that wants a more luxurious toilet paper product, watching a puppy get a manicure, haircut and massage was not an effective trigger.

When the trigger is off target or overwhelming it doesn't help the consumer feel understood and doesn't illicit a call to action, but rather a lack of connection or a defensive withdrawal response.

Taking Aim with the Trigger

Reviewing Rule #2

- **Psychology:** *Humans have a basic, constantly evolving need for physical and emotional supplies, called stimulus hunger.*
- **Translation:** *Triggering a need, wish or anxiety gives your product a reason for being* <u>and</u> *a reason for being the right product for the consumer. Whether your product solves a problem, eases an anxiety or fulfills a fantasy, communicating this attracts the consumer.*

Using Rule #2

It doesn't matter if you're working on a product with a rather low level need or a product that people have just got to have. You must create a trigger and then be aware of the limits around your trigger – how far do you need to push to elicit a response and how far is too far, such that you trigger a negative response and consumers avoid you altogether?

Have you:

1. *Identified what triggers awareness of consumer need, wish or anxiety?*
2. *Found the range (verbal and/or visual cues) in which your trigger can play?*
3. *Identified a weakness in the competition that you can use to your advantage?*
4. *Explored ways to own the trigger? (branding, visual cues, tagline, etc.)*

CHAPTER 3
Supporting Ego Boundaries

---

*"To the degree we're not living our dreams, our comfort zone
has more control of us than we do over ourselves."*
Peter McWilliams

In this Chapter

➤ What are Ego Boundaries?
➤ Breaking down the concept
➤ Examples
➤ How to put your idea to the test

We set our Ego Boundaries based on our individual desire for comfort, security and happiness. Everyday boundaries can include:

✓ *The walls of our house, the fence surrounding our yard.*
✓ *Caller I.D. on our phone.*
✓ *Deciding who to friend or hide on Facebook.*

To make a positive psychological connection, a brand should stay within the Ego Boundaries of their consumers, otherwise you risk alienating them.

What are Ego Boundaries?

In Psychological Terms

Ego Boundary: The internal strength by which a person has an ego barrier to guard his inner space. This is the means the individual uses to screen and interpret the outside world. It is also the structure a person uses to cope with, and modulate his/her interactions with the world." (Bradshaw, 1990, Edith Jacobson, 1964)

Individual Ego Boundaries emerge from the belief that what we want, need, like and dislike is important. Boundaries create a private, secure inner world in which we can be whatever we want to be: free to think, to imagine, to love and to feel. In essence, Ego Boundaries protect a person's ongoing bodily and psychic experience, the "I", the self, one's identity (Federn, 1928).

The goal of having and setting boundaries isn't to build unshakable walls around us, but to gain security and preserve a healthy sense of self that allows us to get close to others without the threat of losing ourselves, being physically at risk or trespassing into the territory of others.

Can your brand be positioned more strongly within consumers' Ego Boundaries than your competition? Conversely, how do you create anxiety about ego boundaries of your competition?

Boundaries are ever changing, influenced by a multitude of forces, including personal relationships, physiological states, life stage, culture, world events and economic factors. In order to choose a product, consumers need to feel that their boundaries are secure. If boundaries are threatened a sense of anxiety is created that becomes an obstacle to messaging, product trial or adoption. Pay attention not just to what makes consumers anxious about your brand and marketing efforts, but what their wishes and "ideal" situations are to firmly place yourself within their boundaries.

For example, a very successful campaign for the Army implored potential recruits to *"Be all you can be."* They wisely did not define what this was, respecting the Ego Boundaries of their target audience, allowing them to imagine what being all you can be might mean solely to them.

18

What are Ego Boundaries?

Translation in Everyday Terms

Everyone has a two dimensional comfort zone that makes up their Ego Boundary – physical boundaries and emotional boundaries.

Boundary: something that indicates or fixes a limit or extent. (Webster Dictionary, 2009)

- **Physical Boundaries.** *When someone enters a crowded elevator there is a moment or two of rippled adjustment as people shift away from the newcomer, away from those who shifted in front of them and so on, trying to create a bubble of space around their bodies. In a crowded commuter train or bus as bodies are piled up against each other like sardines, many people look away or give their attention to something else as they mentally reject the breach to their physical boundaries.*

- **Emotional Boundaries.** *There are many facets to emotional boundaries – anonymity, fantasy, emotional investment, etc. How many times have you hesitated asking a question in a group environment for fear of looking foolish or being told you don't know what you're talking about? And yet, there are ads that ask the consumer to "ask your doctor if Brand X is right for you".*

Can your brand be positioned more strongly within consumers' Ego Boundaries than your competition? Conversely, how do you create anxiety about the ego boundaries of your competition?

Breaking Down the Rule

Making it work for you

Often a marketer doesn't understand Ego Boundaries until they've exposed consumers to their idea, brand, package, product or messaging through research. Why? Because they're too close to the brand/category to consciously feel anxiety. Instead of rationalizing seemingly irrational responses from consumers, take a moment to

Do you know what makes your consumers uncomfortable about using your category? Your brand? Your competition? Is this anxiety related to boundaries?

consider that negative emotional reactions – no matter how trivial sounding – translate into real obstacles to a sale.

One of our recent projects involved helping identify key directions and opportunities in package design for a new wine to be introduced under the Top Chef brand name in conjunction with Terlato Wines International. Since a key element in the Top Chef brand's visual representation was a sharp knife, several designs incorporated images of a knife. Consumer reaction was consistently against prominent use of knives, as many became anxious – *drinking wine when using a knife isn't safe*. The end result used Top Chef's knife, but in a way that contained the image, making it less threatening.

Brands that Made it Work

Foster Farms wanted to convey they don't add water to their chickens to plump them up. Rather than show real chicken parts – which might have grossed some consumers out – they used life-size, mascot-like chickens. Consumers didn't feel violated or overwhelmed by the use of real chickens in the ads. The Ego Boundaries were thus preserved and respected by the brand. This may also have led consumers to believe that respect is also shown to the chickens, which makes the purchase a safer one.

How do you show a 24/7 network without invading the personal space of your consumer? Verizon developed an entire campaign featuring the "Verizon Guy" with an army of technicians available to support their customers in different situations – whether in the kitchen, at a creepy rundown hotel or fixing a bike in the backyard. The supporting network (a legion of people) was never active within the scene. Instead, they were kept in the background, respecting the physical boundaries of the customer featured in the ad (and the viewer at home).

HBO created an ad for their vampire series True Blood. Arguably, this ad isn't for everyone. It featured fangs, blood dripping from mouths and a verse from the song Bad Things. However, Ego Boundaries were maintained wth humor ("*Friends don't let friends drink friends*" slate), sly smiles and sensuality, as vampires delicately wipe blood from their mouths as if it was the most sumptuous delicacy.

How do you dance around cultural sensibilities?

Advertising Hampered by Violating Ego Boundaries

In the Burger King "Wake Up" ad for the Double Crossan'wich™ introduction a man wakes up in his own bed next to the "dude king" who serves him the new breakfast sandwich. This ad triggers the feeling of violation of personal space – *a stranger came into my bed while I was sleeping.*

In a 2009 ad for Boost Mobile, a man and woman are riding on a tandem bike, her brown hair seemingly blowing back on his face. But then she lifts her arm and you realize those long brown locks are armpit hair! Turning to the audience, she asks, "You think this is wrong? It's what other cell-phone companies do to their customers that's wrong." The ick factor is way out of bounds here.

In Yellow Tail wine ran the "Tragedy" ad, intending to spoof opera. However, as the red wine bottle spilled and drained out over the white tablecloth – pooling, dripping and draining onto the floor – and the couple became visibly agitated, the viewer is left feeling incredibly uncomfortable. The imagery comes too close to blood spilling.

Had Yellow Tail approached this idea differently, as did True Blood, it might have been more palatable.

Supporting Ego Boundaries

Reviewing Rule #3

- **Psychology:** *Boundaries create a private, secure inner world in which we can be whatever we want to be. Boundaries are the means an individual uses to screen and interpret the outside world.*
- **Translation:** *Everyone has a two dimensional comfort zone that makes up their Ego Boundary – physical boundaries and emotional boundaries.*

Using Rule #3

To make a positive psychological connection, a brand should stay within their consumers' Ego Boundaries, but first you have to understand those boundaries – both physical and emotional – as they pertain to your brand and message.

Do you:

1. *Know what the physical and emotional ego boundaries related to using your brand, product and category are?*
2. *Know if there is something about the brand, product or category use that makes your consumer uncomfortable and is related to infringement of their boundaries?*
3. *Know if you are flirting with a cultural taboo (e.g., spilling blood)? If so, how can you contain your message so it doesn't invade cultural sensibilities?*
4. *Pay attention to seemingly irrational responses when listening to consumer reactions and try to delve to the emotion behind them?*

CHAPTER 4
Respecting Identity Structures

"To have one's individuality completely ignored is like
being pushed quite out of life
— like being blown out as one blows out a light."
Evelyn Scott

In this Chapter

- ➤ What are Identity Structures?
- ➤ Breaking down the concept
- ➤ Examples
- ➤ How to put your idea to the test

Not only do marketers have to be in tune to consumer needs, but they must be aware of the person the consumer sees themselves as. If the product doesn't fit that self-image, trouble will surely ensue.

✓ Set aside the functional problems with *Premier Smokeless Cigarettes introduced by RJ Reynolds in the late 1980s. For many, part of the smoking experience is the smoke. Take that away and you don't have a smoker.*

✓ *Harley Davidson may have been embraced by Baby Boomers, but that doesn't mean the ruggedly masculine brand could successfully stretch into the perfume market.*

Marketers must design a product, position and brand message that is unique, yet isn't so targeted that they alienate existing franchises or potential markets. Respecting Identity Structures helps them do just that.

What are Identity Structures?

In Psychological Terms

Identity: Whatever makes an entity definable and recognizable, in terms of possessing a set of qualities or characteristics that distinguish it from entities of a different type. (Stanford Encyclopedia of Philosophy, 2006)

Identity structures define how we see ourselves, how we process or perceive information as well as the conscious and unconscious intentions of our actions. There are more permanent elements to identity – *values, intelligence, education, gender, skills/experience* – and more transient attributes that change over time – *memories, relationships, possessions.*

Structural characteristics provide a foundation upon which other aspects of identity are constructed. Some more typical structural characteristics are:

✓ Gender: *which can lead to family roles a consumer takes*

✓ Where raised: *which can influence hobbies, values, fashion, etc.*

✓ Generation born to: *which can create associations with pop culture*

Our identity structure thus is our DNA or essence, and from this structure we can determine what the true motivations of self identity are. These structures are more or less permanent, thus helping us on a deeper level to understand what drives consumer behavior for different demographic groups.

What are Identity Structures?

Translation in Everyday Terms

Unfortunately, there is no one distinguishing Identity Structure of a consumer. Identity Structures are made up of a multitude of factors – self image, demographics, culture, the role consumers play when they use a product and so on.

More about select structural components:

- *A person's self image is their mental picture of themselves, from their ideal physical appearance or age to their personality, skill set and personality. Someone who sees themselves as a proficient driver and a race car fan may balk at the idea of purchasing a mini-van, despite being a father of three.*

- *We play many roles in our daily lives. For example, a woman may be an athlete, wife, mother, friend, career woman, pop culture aficionado, volunteer, and entrepreneur. A woman who is both a wife and a mother may not use her motherly identity structure when buying a new dress for "date night" with her spouse. We are multi-structured creatures.*

Identity: the distinguishing character or personality of an individual. (Webster Dictionary, 2009)

To explore Identity Structures, ask: What do you believe people think about you when you use Brand X?

An accountant who wears a suit to work every day morphs into a Son of Anarchy, gunning a vintage Harley past lumbering RVs on the weekend. How do you define him?

Breaking Down Identity Structures

Making it work for you

It's popular to segment markets into different attitude or user groups, but we would argue you get more bang for your marketing buck if you find a common denominator – a common Identity Structure – among your users. Nike has been extremely successful tapping into the worldwide desire to be a standout. By communicating that their brand is for those who pursue excellence with perseverance and style, they've been able to

What are the common roles – real or imagined – that your consumers share?

transcend boundaries of ability, age and culture. They may have started out as a running shoe, but they quickly became both a performance and a fashion icon. Knowing your consumers' more common identity structures and using them in

What are the shared dreams or emotions tied to product use?

your brand's position/communication help create a feeling of consumer inclusion that is very powerful.

Not everyone can offer a customized product like avatars on the Wii. When consumers are segmented and tightly marketed to by usage behavior, category benefit or consumer group, someone will invariable feel left out. When the common ground – no matter how narrow – is overlooked, marketers risk alienating someone because they can no longer identify with the product. The trick is to find the common ground among most or all users without becoming just like everyone else, while staying true to the brand premise.

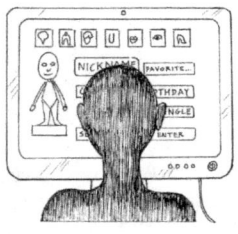

Brands that Made it Work

Just for Men tagline: "Stay in the Game."

Just for Men hair color recently ran two different commercials in a campaign designed to appeal to a man's need to look as energetic and vital as he feels without discounting the wisdom he's earned along with his grey hair. In one ad, two daughters tell their single dad that it's time to color his hair and – *voila!* – he gets a date. In another ad, a man is about to be interviewed for a job. He appears both as his current grey haired self on one end of the couch and as himself with all grey completely covered on the other. The compromise? The men merge in the middle to a man with grey accented hair. The common ground was the desire to look younger, but Just for Men acknowledged there were (at least) two different user groups to appeal to.

During the most recent recession it seemed like FreeCreditReport.com dominated the airwaves. Each television spot got viewers singing along with three men as they tried to recover from lives damaged because they didn't keep a close enough eye on their credit. The shared experiences that might be improved if one had kept up with their credit score range from major purchases – buying a house, buying a car – to minor ones – buying a cell phone.

Advertising Violating Identity Structures

Whenever brands unintentionally violate or abandon their target consumer they are violating the identity structures of this group, a violation which cannot be tolerated. For example, when British Airways attempted to reach business travelers in their Club World print campaign, they tried to connect through their consumer's identity that as world weary travelers they should be treated as someone important, pampered and special. They meant to offset the cramped and helpless feelings of traveling on planes today. In the campaign, from the waist up the traveler is a photograph of a grown man, but from the waist down the traveler is a baby in a diaper. While British Airways was attempting to convey the luxury and pampering we often receive as children, they violated the identity structure of their target user by implying that the man's lower extremities

were like that of a baby – not good for conveying the omnipotence of the business traveler.

When Holiday Inn remodeled their properties, they wanted to show people they'd upgraded and moved the brand in a different and unexpected direction, so they created the Sex Change ad. The ad featured a man at his high school reunion, who was then revealed to be a woman (in a leopard print cocktail dress), having undergone a sex change operation. The brand unintentionally may have violated their consumers' perceived view of themselves resulting in heightened anxiety and withdrawal from Holiday Inn in order to stay safe within their preexisting identity structures.

Respecting Identity Structures

Reviewing Rule #4

- **Psychology:** *Identity structures define how we see ourselves, how we process or perceive information, as well as the conscious and unconscious intentions of our actions. There are more permanent elements to identity – values, intelligence, education, gender, skills/ experience – and more transient attributes that change over time – memories, relationships, possessions.*
- **Translation:** *There is no one distinguishing Identity Structure of a consumer. Identity Structures are made up of a multitude of factors – self image, demographics, culture, the role consumers play when they use a product and so on.*

Using Rule #4

If marketers cannot personalize their message, they need to uncover the common DNA of their consumers' identity structure. In doing so they can appeal across demographic and user groups.

Put your brand/communication to the test:

1. *Can you personalize your product or message?*
2. *If not, have you looked beneath the surface of brand and category use to find shared experiences?*
3. *What underlying identities do your consumers have in common?*
4. *Does your communication fit your consumers' view of themselves?*

CHAPTER 5
Providing the Good Fit

"We must learn to balance the material wonders of technology
with the spiritual demands of our human race."
John Naisbitt

In this Chapter

> What is the Good Fit?
> Breaking down the concept
> Examples
> How to put your idea to the test

We've all experienced that euphoria when everything went "just right". Maybe you cooked a fabulous Thanksgiving dinner and everyone attending got along, someone helped you do the dishes and now you're feeling full and happy as you watch whatever you want on T.V.

✓ **Tickle Me Elmo.** *In 1996, Tickle Me Elmo became the must-have toy of the holiday season. How did Tyco Toys pull that off against Nintendo 64, Holiday Barbie and Star Wars figurines? With a cute, chubby plush toy, accessible packaging (buyers could touch him, shake him and make him laugh), a PR* *campaign to create pre-release buzz among the media and a sweet television campaign that was pulled after the first month due to skyrocketing demand for the product.*

✓ **Garlic Cake.** *On the other hand, Gunderson & Rosario, Inc. introduced Garlic Cake about twenty years ago. They thought the product would be great served as an hors d'oevre with spreads and meats. Neither the packaging nor any promotion conveyed this "greatness" to consumers.*

Brands should strive to communicate the feeling of being "just right" – providing a physical experience/presence that fits while meeting emotional needs.

What is the Good Fit?

In Psychological Terms

Good Fit: The good fit psychologically is achieving a balance or synchronicity between a person's physical emotional self and the outer environment. A person thus achieves a sense of harmony inside and outside. (Heinz Hartmann, Ego Psychology and the Problem of Adaptation, 1939)

An individual interacts with his/her external environment, while simultaneously responding to internal forces. The Good Fit is achieved when a person feels a sense of comfort or integration between often conflicting elements within or outside of that person. Initial mechanisms of integration develop in infancy and become more sophisticated as a child matures, becoming defenses that often shut out people, objects and messages that are not a Good Fit.

Achieving a Good Fit can overcome consumer defense mechanisms and increase the likelihood of trial. Ask yourself:

Do the physical features of your brand support the emotional benefits?

✓ Is there a good fit between the physical supplies (i.e., physical features) and emotional supplies (ie., emotional benefits) being offered by a brand? *Don't tell us you've never pondered the value of a store brand against its lack of brand cred, especially when considering which brand of potato chips to take to a party.*

✓ Does the brand offer synchronicity or balance between a person's inside and social self? *In the past 10 years there has been a trend in grocery stores to license their coffee bar to coffee houses such as Seattle's Best and Starbucks. Why? Although the quality of the coffee was good and a good value, carrying around a store brand cup of coffee wasn't as socially acceptable around the conference room.*

Does your product or message project who your target wants to be? Real versus ideal self.

✓ Is there a good fit offered by the brand balancing the consumer's intellectual and emotional life? *Consider the challenges of hybrid vehicles, which first came onto the scene with decidedly different body styles than their gas powered counterparts. The need to be environmentally responsible and save on gas bills was appealing, but there was a strong emotional need not to be lumped in with the fringe environmentalists that marketers hadn't accounted for.*

Is your product or message in line with people/groups your consumer identifies with?

When a Good Fit is lacking, a defense mechanism is put into place. How strong this obstacle to purchase is depends upon the level of integration of elements/reduction of anxiety within your target consumer.

Has your target put up emotional defense mechanisms against your brand, product or category?

What is the Good Fit?
Translation In Everyday Terms

Like Goldilocks, the Good Fit is about achieving that connection where everything is just right. If a brand can communicate this feeling, many

Fit: to be suitable for or to harmonize with. (Webster Dictionary, 2009)

obstacles to purchase (intellectual alibis) will be removed, reducing the perceived risk of purchase and perhaps creating an avalanche of demand.

Despite pundits who felt limited 3G coverage and short battery life were deal breakers, the iPhone was an immediate runaway success. Why? It built on the cool factor of the iPod, made you more productive, filled up your free time and was easy to use – all in a sleek black case that could be covered with a "skin" to further express your individuality. The iPhone was introduced with a television teaser called "Hello", which was a montage of movie clips with actors saying, "Hello," followed by a picture of the iPhone. Did it tout product benefits? No. It didn't need to say more with the buzz surrounding it. Who wanted the iPhone? Only everyone.

Breaking Down the Rule
Making it work for you

Creating a fabulous product doesn't guarantee success. Many great products fail. Communication is often necessary to overcome psychological barriers to purchase and reinforce that the brand offers good emotional benefits and physical features.

Talk about the positive attributes of your brand using evocative language that emphasizes the emotional benefits.

Let's say you are marketing jeans to women that make them look like they are a size smaller. A pair of jeans that visually slims you down is a miracle. Every woman should buy a pair (or 5!), right? But other companies have introduced jeans like this without huge success. So you do your homework. You know your target and the obstacles or anxieties they have toward the category and your brand.

When asked, the target (women, age 25-49) might say that they want good fitting jeans that accentuate their shape. When probed further they might reveal they want comfortable jeans that make them look younger and slimmer, as well as revealing that their fear in buying a pair of jeans is that it will make them look old and fat!

Not only does your target want to look slimmer, but they worry that they're actual shape isn't the same as it was when they were 18! With this knowledge, you can bring it all together to make sure that the physical attributes of your jeans compliment the emotional ones. Featuring a younger, albeit slightly curvier, woman in your communication is more likely to provide the emotional reward that is sought – a Good Fit!

During the latest recession, consumers were worried about their bank balance, but still had the urge to buy the latest in fashion, brand or technology. How did they balance value against need? Self-image against practicality? Enter the smaller size product – smaller wine containers, smaller Gucci bags, a smaller version of the iPod. Marketers scrambled to find the Good Fit in financially challenging times.

Just because they say they can't afford you now doesn't mean you can't come up with a creative way to meet the demand for your product.

Brands that Made it Work

Hewlett-Packard wanted to increase laptop sales among women, but knew that meant more than just covering an existing PC in a hot pink plastic case. So marketing executives contacted couture clothing designer Vivienne Tam. Ms. Tam seized on the smaller HP Mini Netbook as the perfect form factor for her "digital clutch" design. The HP Mini has soft corners, keys like a

piano, champagne-colored metal and a fashionable exterior. Instead of using traditional media, the HP Mini Netbook was introduced as a featured accessory in Ms. Tam's fashion shows worldwide. The product sold five times more than its forecast and was considered by many to be a hot product of 2009. Another Good Fit.

During the recent recession, DiGiorno gained sales and share in the competitive frozen pizza category by positioning itself against delivery brands, like Domino's and Pizza Hut. Combining its DiGiornonomics campaign (*"It's not delivery. It's DiGirono!"*), fulfilling the brand promise of good taste at a good value and providing quality SKUs beyond your traditional pepperoni and sausage was a Good Fit for cash strapped consumers.

Rogaine conducted psychological research on its hair growth formula and learned that its primary customer was one who needed to feel special and desirable. Their ads associated the use of Rogaine with attracting women. Sales rose greatly during this campaign since they were able to create a good fit between the physical deliverable of the product (growing men's hair back) and the emotional benefit of the product (hair as a powerful trigger of sexual attraction).

Advertising Lacking the Good Fit

In the beginning of 2010, Taco Bell introduced a campaign meant to target those with healthier eating habits – the Taco Bell Drive Thru Diet. The ads and tie-ins met with skepticism and derision. Historically, Taco Bell targeted teens and young men – a cohort you don't normally associate with watching their waistline. This departure was viewed as a betrayal among their target consumers, not to mention the question of believability by those trying to eat healthier and slim down. Taco Bell, a brand that usually is spot on with its target, did not achieve a Good Fit with their Drive Thru Diet.

In 2010, Kia ran an ad with the cast of "Yo Gabba Gabba", a children's show. In the spot the beloved children's characters dream of taking the family car. During their wild ride, they stop to get a tattoo, sit in a hot tub with a beautiful woman and party in Las Vegas. The ad ends with a child sitting in the backseat of the Kia with the Yo Gabba Gabba toys and the mom driving them away. Is the mom supposed to feel wild and young again with this car? Or is the ad targeted to future drivers as it tries to create a fun, hip image for Kia? Neither seems a Good Fit.

Providing the Good Fit
Reviewing Rule #5
- **Psychology:** *The good fit psychologically is achieving a balance or synchronicity between a person's physical emotional self and the outer environment.*
- **Translation:** *Like Goldilocks, the Good Fit is about achieving that connection where everything feels just right.*

Using Rule #5

Every element of the brand and its communication should strive for a balance of physical needs, psychological wants, moral compass and social constraints – to create the feeling of a Good Fit.

Do you know:

1. *If the physical features of your brand support the emotional benefits?*
2. *If your product or message projects who your target wants to be?*
3. *If your product or message is in line with people/ groups your consumer wants to identify with?*
4. *If your target has put up emotional defense mechanisms against your brand/product/category?*

5 Rules of Consumer Engagement
Overview

As you embark on a new project or develop your brand's web, point-of-sale, advertising campaign or any other communication, reference the 5 Rules of Consumer Engagement. In doing so you can reach a deeper understanding of your consumer, identify the hot buttons that might turn them on or off and create an emotional bond with your brand that leads to reduced obstacles to trial, higher loyalty and, ultimately, stronger sales.

Rule 1: Getting into Empathic Attunement
1. *Establish the feeling that the brand understands the consumer or segment.*
2. *Prioritize the meeting of needs, wishes and anxieties in your presentation.*
3. *Provide cues (both verbally and visually) that align with your consumer's sense of self.*
4. *Address an important concern, fear or anxiety without overwhelming the consumer.*

Rule 2: Pulling the Trigger
1. *Identify what triggers consumer awareness of the need, wish or anxiety.*
2. *Find the range (verbal, visual) in which your trigger can play.*
3. *Identify a weakness in the competition and use it to your advantage.*
4. *Establish ownership of the trigger (branding, visual cues, tagline, etc.).*

Rule 3: Supporting Ego Boundaries
Identify the physical and emotional ego boundaries related to using your brand, product and category.

Become familiar with what about the brand, product or category use makes your consumer uncomfortable, especially if it is related to infringement of their boundaries.

If flirting with a cultural taboo (e.g., spilling blood), know how you can contain your message so it doesn't invade cultural sensibilities.

Pay attention to seemingly irrational consumer responses.

Rule 4: Respecting Identity Structures

1. Try to personalize your product or message.
2. If you can't personalize the message, look beneath the surface of brand and category use to find shared experiences.
3. Explore underlying identities that your consumers have in common.
4. Test that your communication fits the consumer's view of themselves.

Rule 5: Providing the Good Fit

1. Physical features of your brand should support the emotional benefits you communicate.
2. Your product or message should project who your target wants to be.
3. Your product or message should be in line with people/groups your target identifies with.
4. Identify emotional defense mechanisms your target has put up against your brand/category.

www.ingramcontent.com/pod-product-compliance
Lightning Source LLC
Chambersburg PA
CBHW051252170526
45165CB00004B/1681